Theory and Sightreading for Singers

LEVEL 2
Second Edition

The EM Music Voice Method Series

Written by

Elizabeth Irene Hames
and Michelle Anne Blumsack

Distributed by:

EM Music Publishing
5608 Oakmont Ln.
Fort Worth, TX 76112
EM.MusicPublishing@gmail.com

emmusicpublishing.com

© 2015 EM Music Publishing
All rights reserved.

Preface

This book provides a progressive curriculum for intermediate theory and sightreading intended to follow completion of *Theory and Sightreading for Singers Level 1*. It can be used in a classroom setting or as a complement to private study. The material is intended for middle-school aged students and older.

Each lesson provides instruction on theory, a worksheet to reinforce the concepts, and a sightreading exercise to provide practical application of those concepts. Each of the book's five units contains three lessons as well as a unit quiz. A downloadable answer key is available at www.emmusicpublishing.com under Our Books>Free Resources.

This second edition corrects minor errors and is fully compatible with the first edition.

Table of Contents

Unit 1..1
- Lesson 1: Review of Note Names and Ledger Lines..................................2
- Lesson 2: Note Value Review, Intro to 16th –Notes and Ties...................5
- Lesson 3: Time Signature and Key Signature Review.............................8
- Unit 1 Quiz..11

Unit 2..12
- Lesson 4: Whole and Half Steps; the Major Scale.................................13
- Lesson 5: Minor Keys..16
- Lesson 6: Different Forms of the Minor Scale....................................19
- Unit 2 Quiz..23

Unit 3..24
- Lesson 7: Simple Meter vs. Compound Meter.......................................25
- Lesson 8: Musical Road Signs..29
- Lesson 9: Interval Quality...34
- Unit 3 Quiz..37

Unit 4..38
- Lesson 10: Introduction to Chords...39
- Lesson 11: Intervals Greater than a 5th...42
- Lesson 12: Tonic and Dominant..45
- Unit 4 Quiz..49

Unit 5..50
- Lesson 13: Supertonic and Subdominant..51
- Lesson 14: The Chromatic Scale..54
- Lesson 15: Roman Numerals in Minor...57
- Unit 5 Quiz..60

Final Review..61

Appendix A: Key Signatures..64
Appendix B: Scales...65

Glossary..68

Unit 1

- Lesson 1: Review of Note Names and Ledger Lines
- Lesson 2: Note Value Review, Intro to 16th-Notes and Ties
- Lesson 3: Time Signature and Key Signature Review
- Unit 1 Quiz

Lesson 1
Review of Note Names and Ledger Lines

In Level 1, you learned the letter names of the notes of the treble clef:

E   G   B   D   F   F   A   C   E
Every Good Boy Does Fine

and the bass clef:

G   B   D   F   A   A   C   E   G
Great Big Dogs Fight Animals   All Cows Eat Grass

You also learned that a **ledger line** is a special line used for notes written below or above the staff. Ledger lines can be used with any clef on any staff:

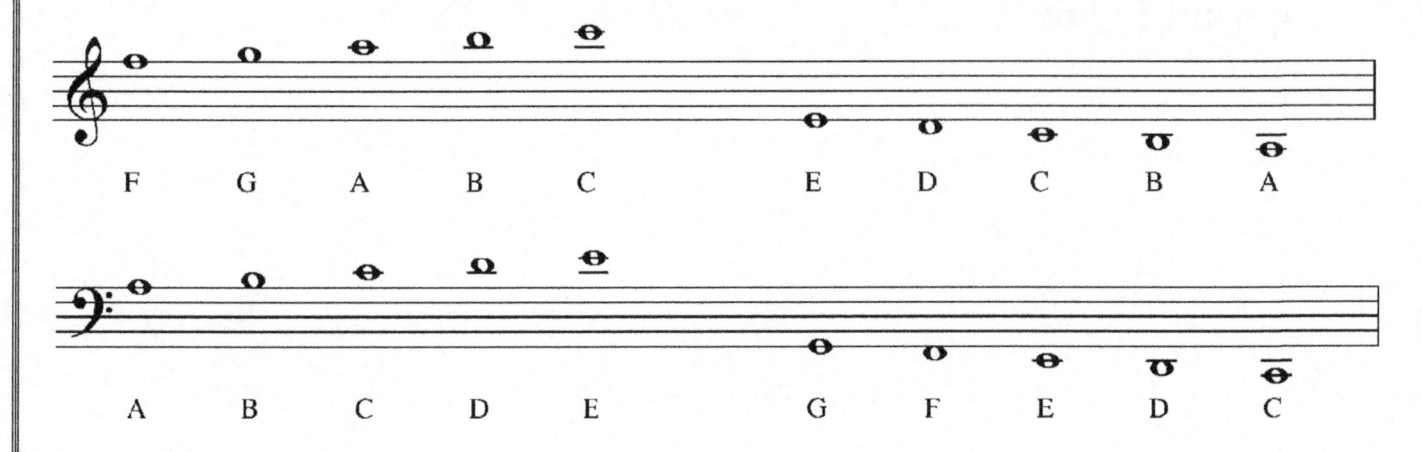

F   G   A   B   C   E   D   C   B   A

A   B   C   D   E   G   F   E   D   C

It is possible to continue moving further above or below the staff by adding more ledger lines as needed.

2

Worksheet 1
Review of Note Names and Ledger Lines

Complete the following sentences:

The line notes of the treble clef are ___ , ___ , ___ , ___ , and ___ .

The space notes of the treble clef are ___ , ___ , ___ , and ___ .

The line notes of the bass clef are ___ , ___ , ___ , ___ , and ___ .

The space notes of the bass clef are ___ , ___ , ___ , and ___ .

A _____ _____ is a special line used for notes written below or above the staff.

Identify the treble clef notes below:

Identify the bass clef notes below:

Draw each indicated pitch using only ledger line notes:

C   A   B   F   E   G   E   C   D   F   B

Sightreading 1

Note that each of the following examples contains ledger lines. Sing through the melodies with your teacher in a comfortable range.

Lesson 2
Note Value Review, Intro to 16th-Notes and Ties

Below are the types of notes you learned about in Level 1 and their values. Remember that when a dot is added to a note, half of the original value is added to its length.

Symbol	Name	Value
♪ ♪.	Eighth Note/Dotted Eighth Note	½ beat / ¾ beat
♩ ♩.	Quarter Note/Dotted Quarter Note	1 beat / 1 ½ beats
♩ ♩.	Half Note/Dotted Half Note	2 beats / 3 beats
o o.	Whole Note/Dotted Whole Note	4 beats / 6 beats

One new type of note we will be using in this book is the **sixteenth note.** A sixteenth note receives one-fourth of a beat, meaning that there are four sixteenth notes in one beat. One method of counting with sixteenth notes is to insert *e + a* ("ee-and-uh") to show the notes that occur between beats. Sixteenth notes written separately look like eighth notes with an extra flag. Two or more sixteenth notes can be joined together by a double beam.

A marking that affects the length of the note is a **tie,** a curved line that joins together two or more notes on the same line or space. Tied notes act as a single note that is to be held for the value of the notes added together. Note that the tie looks very similar to the slur marking, but a slur is placed over or under notes of different pitches.

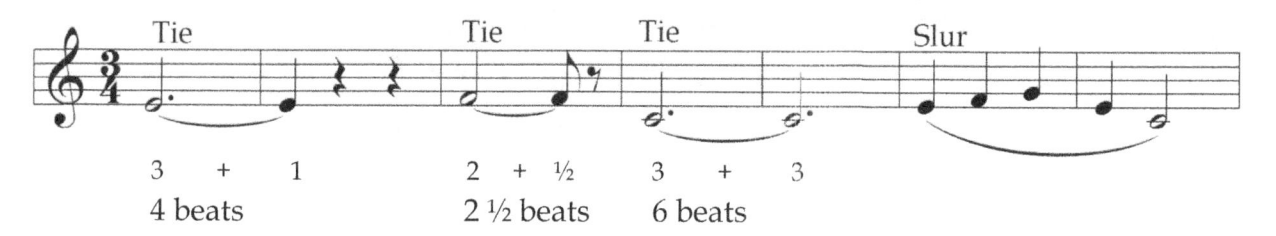

Worksheet 2
Note Value Review, Intro to 16th-Notes and Ties

Complete the chart below:

Symbol	Name	Value
	Sixteenth Note	
♪		
	Dotted Whole Note	
		3 beats
♩		

Figure out the durations of the following tied notes:

1. ♩ ♪ = _____ beats

2. ♩ ♪ = _____ beats

3. o͜ o = _____ beats

4. o͜ ♩ ♪ = _____ beats

5. ♩. ♩ = _____ beats

6. ♩ o ♩. = _____ beats

Write in the counts for each melody on Sightreading 2 (next page). The example below shows the counts for melody #1.

    1 2 3 + 4   1 e + a 2 + 3 4   1 2 3 + 4   1 e + a 2 + 3 4

Sightreading 2

Clap and count the rhythm of each melody out loud before singing it through on solfege.

Lesson 3
Time Signature and Key Signature Review

Remember from Level 1 that the number of beats in a measure is determined by the **time signature.** Time signatures are written with two numbers and look like a fraction:

4 The top 4 shows that each measure will have 4 beats.

4 The bottom 4 shows that a quarter (or 1/4) note equals 1 beat.

The time signatures you have seen so far have had a 4 for the bottom number, showing that the quarter note will receive one beat. This is the most common. However, any type of note can establish "the beat." For example, a piece of music with the time signature 4/2 will have 4 beats per measure with the half (or 1/2) note receiving one beat, and a piece of music with the time signature of 3/8 will have 3 beats per measure with the eighth (or 1/8) note receiving one beat.

You may also remember from Level 1 that a **key signature** is a set of sharps or flats that denotes the key of a piece of music. A key signature that contains no sharps or flats indicates the key of C Major. Otherwise, use the following rules:

For a flat key:
If the key signature has one flat, the key is "F." If the key has more than one flat, name the *next to last flat*.

Key of F   Key of Bb   Key of Eb   Key of Ab

For a sharp key:
Name the *last sharp* and go up one letter name.

Key of G   Key of D   Key of A   Key of E

Another way to determine keys is to name the last flat as "Fa" or the last sharp as "Ti."

See Appendix A for a reference guide to all the key signatures.

Did you know?
Every key signature has two possible keys: a major and a relative minor. The keys discussed above are major. We will discuss minor keys in a future lesson.

Worksheet 3
Time Signature and Key Signature Review

1. How many beats per measure are in 3/2 time? _____

   What kind of note will receive one beat? _____

2. How many beats per measure are in 4/8 time? _____

   What kind of note will receive one beat? _____

3. What key contains no sharps or flats? _____

For each of the following, add a correct time signature and determine the key. Note that multiple time signatures could be used for certain examples.

a.

Key of _____

b.

Key of _____

c.

Key of _____

d.

Key of _____

Sightreading 3

Some of the following examples contain time signatures that you may not have seen before. After noting the time signature, determine the key for each example then sing it through with your teacher.

1. Key of _____

2. Key of _____

3. Key of _____

4. Key of _____

Unit 1 Quiz

Identify the following key signatures:

1. _____ 2. _____ 3. _____ 4. _____ 5. _____ 6. _____

Determine the durations of the following tied notes:

1. = _____ beats
2. = _____ beats
3. = _____ beats
4. = _____ beats
5. = _____ beats
6. = _____ beats

Identify the following bass clef pitches:

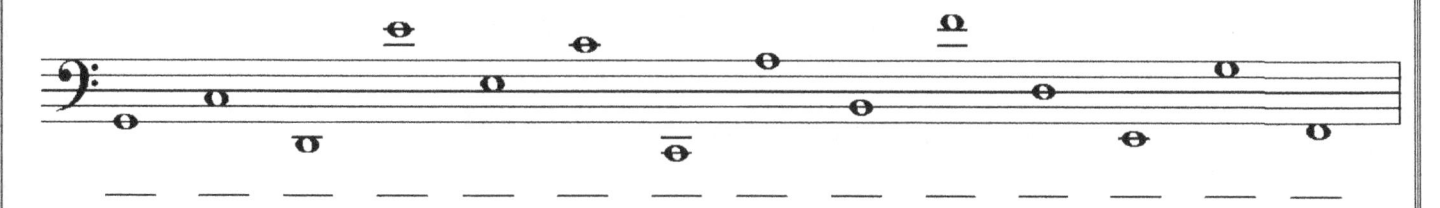

Identify the following treble clef pitches:

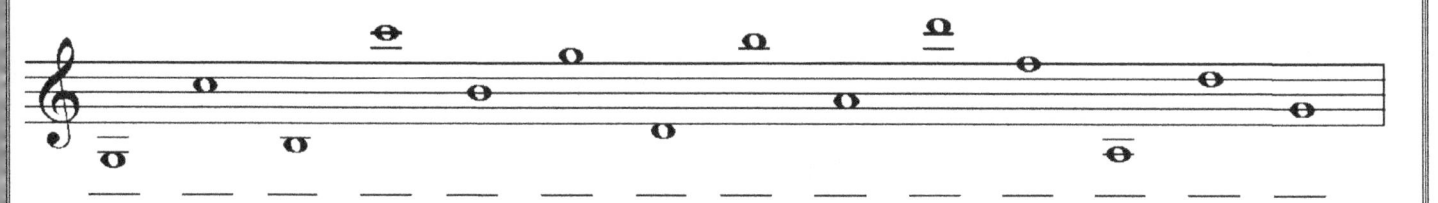

Note the time signature and add barlines to the following example. Don't forget to add a double barline at the end.

Unit 2

- Lesson 4: Whole and Half Steps; the Major Scale
- Lesson 5: Minor Keys
- Lesson 6: Different Forms of the Minor Scale
- Unit 2 Quiz

Lesson 4
Whole and Half Steps; the Major Scale

In the last book we talked about steps (or 2nds), when a note moves up or down to the note next to it. There are two different kinds of steps: **whole steps** and **half steps**, also known as **Major 2nds** and **minor 2nds**.

If you look at a piano keyboard, a half step is when a note moves to the very next note, for example C up to D♭, A down to G#, or B up to C. A whole step is the same as two half steps combined and has one note in between, such as C up to D, B down to A, or E up to F#.

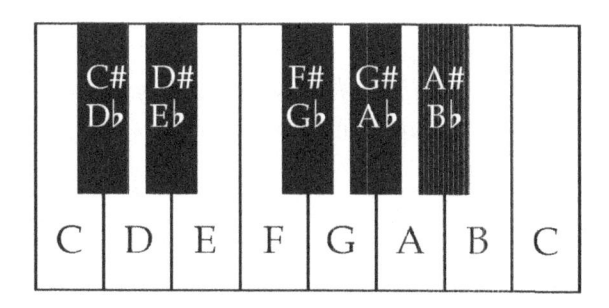

You learned before that a **scale** is a collection of pitches. The most common type of scale is the **Major Scale**. The major scale is made up of a pattern of whole and half steps. The pattern for the major scale is 2 whole steps, 1 half step, 3 whole steps, and 1 more half step. You can see this pattern of whole steps (W) and half steps (H) in the C Major scale below:

The same pattern can be used starting on any note to form a major scale. Notice in the D Major scale below that F# and C# have to be added to keep the pattern of whole and half steps. Also notice that each note is written on a separate line or space. Because of this, F# and C# are used instead of G♭ and D♭. This is why different key signatures are necessary for different keys.

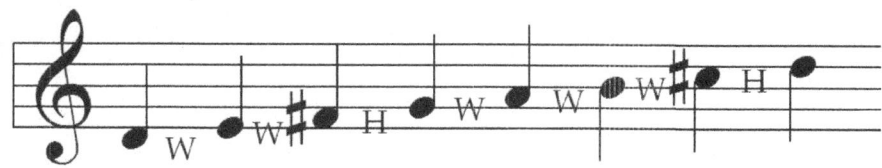

You should already be quite familiar with the sound of the major scale. The solfege scale that you have been singing is also a major scale.

13

Worksheet 4
Whole and Half Steps; the Major Scale

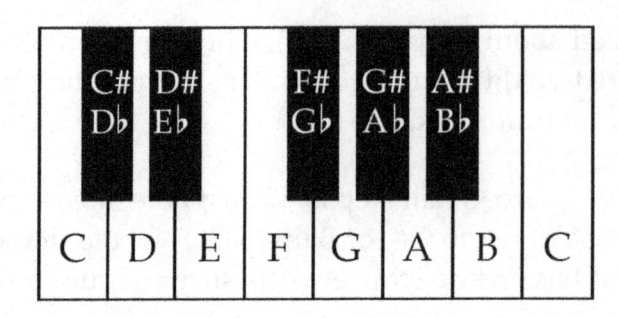

On the staff below, write the note which is a half step above each note shown. Use the keyboard graphic as a reference.

On the staff below, write the note which is a whole step below each note shown.

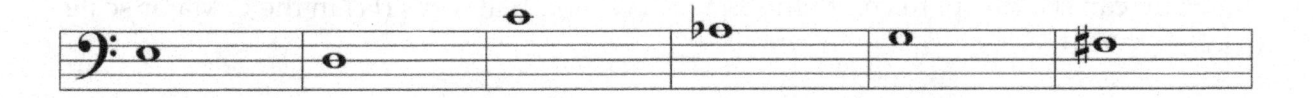

Write out the F Major scale. Be sure to include any necessary flats or sharps.

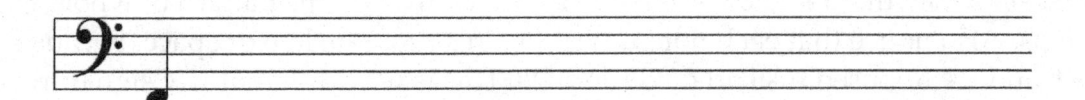

Write out the A Major scale. Be sure to include any necessary flats or sharps.

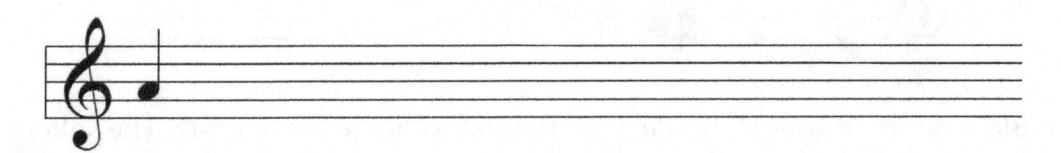

Sightreading 4

For each example, first sing through the appropriate major scale with your teacher. Next clap and count the rhythm out loud, and then sing the melody using solfege.

1. Key of _____

2. Key of _____

3. Key of _____

4. Key of _____

Lesson 5
Minor Keys

Have you ever noticed that most Christmas music sounds quite different from most Halloween music? You might describe their respective qualities as bright versus dark, or happy versus sad. In lesson 4, you learned about the major scale. This scale has a brighter and happier quality to it than the **minor scale**. Sing through the following two examples with your teacher to hear the difference.

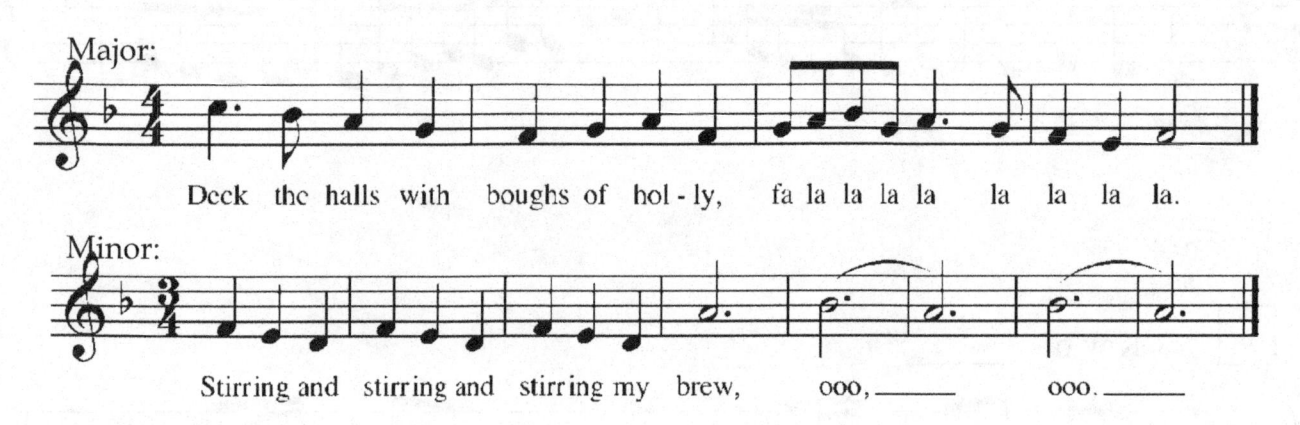

Major:

Deck the halls with boughs of hol-ly, fa la la la la la la la la.

Minor:

Stirring and stirring and stirring my brew, ooo,_____ ooo._____

You may have noticed that the key signature is the same for both examples. So what makes them sound so different? Each major key has a **relative minor** key. The minor key has the same key signature as its relative major but a different **tonal center**. The tonal center of a piece of music is the note that feels like home. In solfege, the tonal center is "Do."

To determine a minor key from a key signature, first identify the major key according to the key signature rules you learned. Then go down the interval of a minor third (three half steps) to determine the minor key.

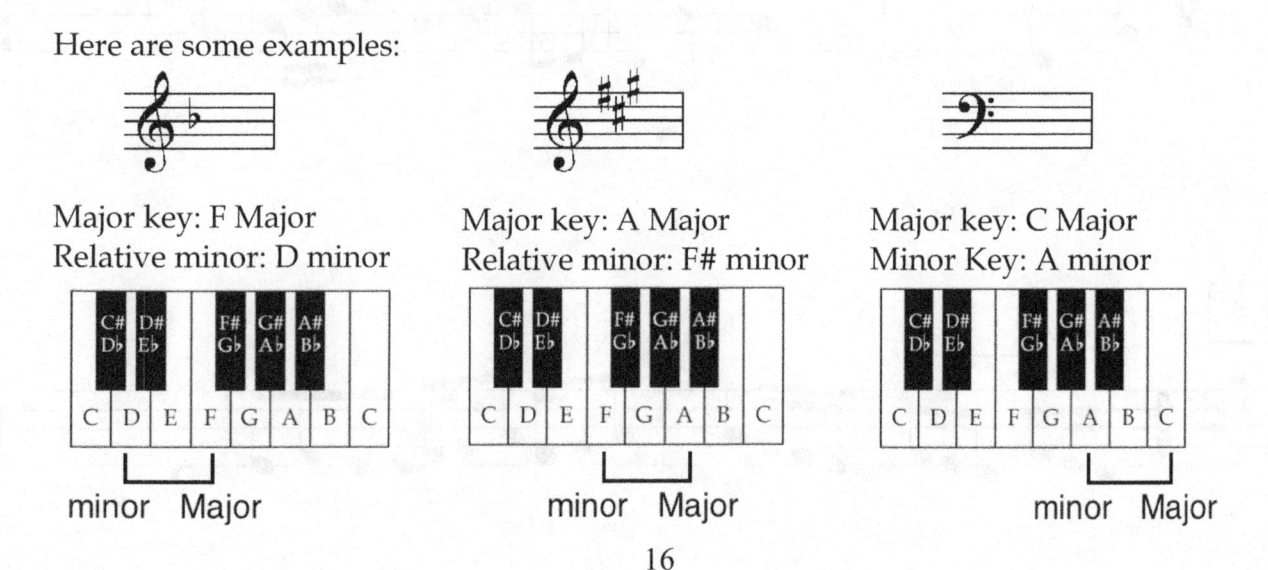

Here are some examples:

Major key: F Major
Relative minor: D minor

Major key: A Major
Relative minor: F# minor

Major key: C Major
Minor Key: A minor

Worksheet 5
Minor Keys

Complete the following sentences:

1. Music that is bright and happy like most Christmas music is in a _____ key.

2. Music that has a dark, sad quality is in a _____ key.

3. Two keys that share the same key signature but have different tonal centers are called _____.

4. The note a third down from G is _____.

5. A third down from _____ is D.

6. The note a third down from D is _____.

For each of the following key signatures, identify both the major and minor keys.

___ Major   ___ Major   ___ Major   ___ Major
___ minor   ___ minor   ___ minor   ___ minor

___ Major   ___ Major   ___ Major   ___ Major
___ minor   ___ minor   ___ minor   ___ minor

Sightreading 5

Each of the following examples has been given to you twice: once in a major key and once in its relative minor. You will notice that two versions of the solfege for the minor examples have been given. Some teachers prefer to use "La-Based" minor solfege and some prefer to use "Do-Based" minor. You will learn more about these systems in the next lesson. For now, use whichever your teacher prefers.

1a Key of _____ Major

1b Key of _____ minor

La-based: La Ti Do Re   Do Do Ti La   Ti Do Re Mi Re   Do Ti La Ti Do Re   Do Ti La
Do-based: Do Re Me Fa   Me Me Re Do   Re Me Fa Sol Fa   Me Re Do Re Me Fa   Me Re Do

2a Key of _____ Major

2b Key of _____ minor

La-based: La Do Mi Fa   Mi Mi La   Mi Fa Mi Re   Do Do Re Mi   Re Do Ti Do Ti   La La
Do-based: Do Me Sol Le   Sol Sol Do   Sol Le So Fa   Me Me Fa Sol   Fa Me Re Me Re   Do Do

18

Lesson 6
Different Forms of the Minor Scale

As mentioned in Sightreading 5, there are two different systems of solfege for minor keys. "La-Based Minor" uses "La" as its tonal center, the note of a key that feels like home, and maintains the solfege relationships from the major scale. "Do-Based Minor" uses "Do" as its tonal center and uses solfege alterations to show the differences between major and minor. You will see both systems demonstrated in this lesson. Your teacher will instruct you on his or her preference.

There are several versions of the minor scale commonly found in music. They each have different purposes. The simplest of these is the **natural minor scale**, which contains only notes found in the key signature. The pattern of half/whole steps, along with both sets of solfege, is shown below in C minor:

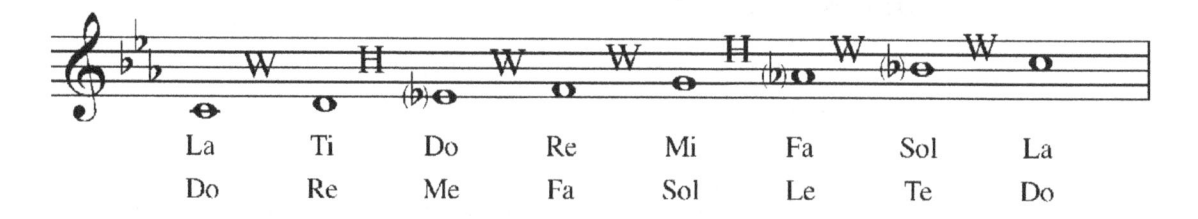

| La | Ti | Do | Re | Mi | Fa | Sol | La |
| Do | Re | Me | Fa | Sol | Le | Te | Do |

One variant of the minor scale is the **harmonic minor scale.** The harmonic minor scale has a raised 7th scale degree. Raising the 7th scale degree impacts the resulting harmonies, which is why it is called the harmonic minor scale. To raise the 7th, you will use either a sharp or a **natural sign** (♮), which cancels out a sharp or flat. In La-Based minor, "Sol" becomes "Si," and in Do-Based minor, "Te" becomes "Ti." When singing the harmonic minor scale, be careful of the awkward interval between the 6th and 7th scale degrees.

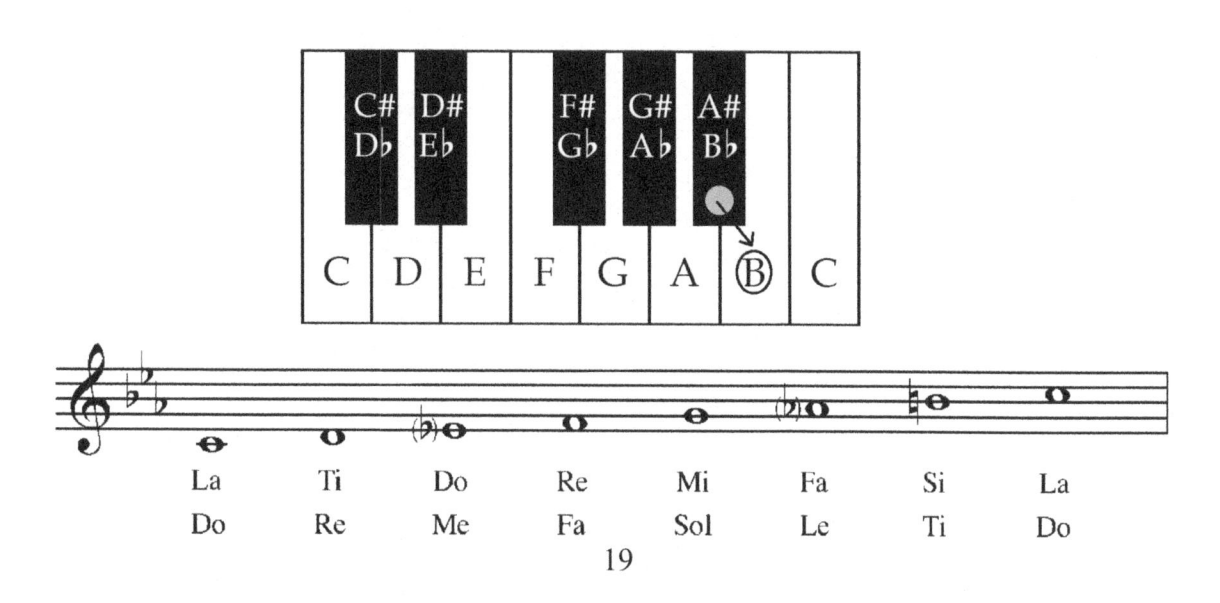

| La | Ti | Do | Re | Mi | Fa | Si | La |
| Do | Re | Me | Fa | Sol | Le | Ti | Do |

Another variant of minor is the **melodic minor scale.** Unlike the natural and harmonic minor scales, melodic minor is different ascending (going up) than it is descending (going down). Ascending, the 6th and 7th scale degrees are raised. (In La-Based minor, "Fa" becomes "Fi" and "Sol" becomes "Si." In Do-Based minor, "Le" becomes "La" and "Te" becomes "Ti.") The descending melodic minor scale is identical to the natural minor scale. The melodic minor scale was invented so that the raised 7th scale degree could be used while avoiding the awkward interval between the 6th and 7th scale degrees that occurs in harmonic minor. The raised 7th is primarily used to lead up to the tonal center, so the raised 6th and 7th are not necessary when descending in melodic minor.

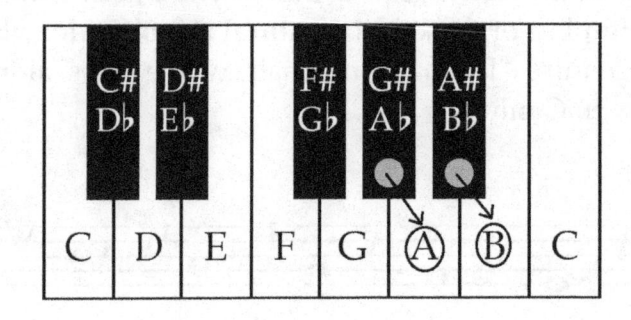

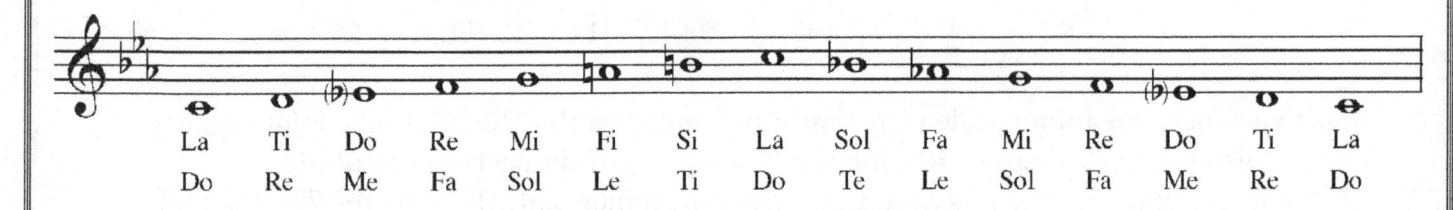

| La | Ti | Do | Re | Mi | Fi | Si | La | Sol | Fa | Mi | Re | Do | Ti | La |
| Do | Re | Me | Fa | Sol | Le | Ti | Do | Te | Le | Sol | Fa | Me | Re | Do |

Worksheet 6
Different Forms of the Minor Scale

For each pair of staves, first use the given note as a starting pitch and draw a major scale using sharps or flats as needed. Next, determine the relative minor and draw a natural minor scale on the second staff. Last, write in the solfege for each scale according to your teacher's preferences.

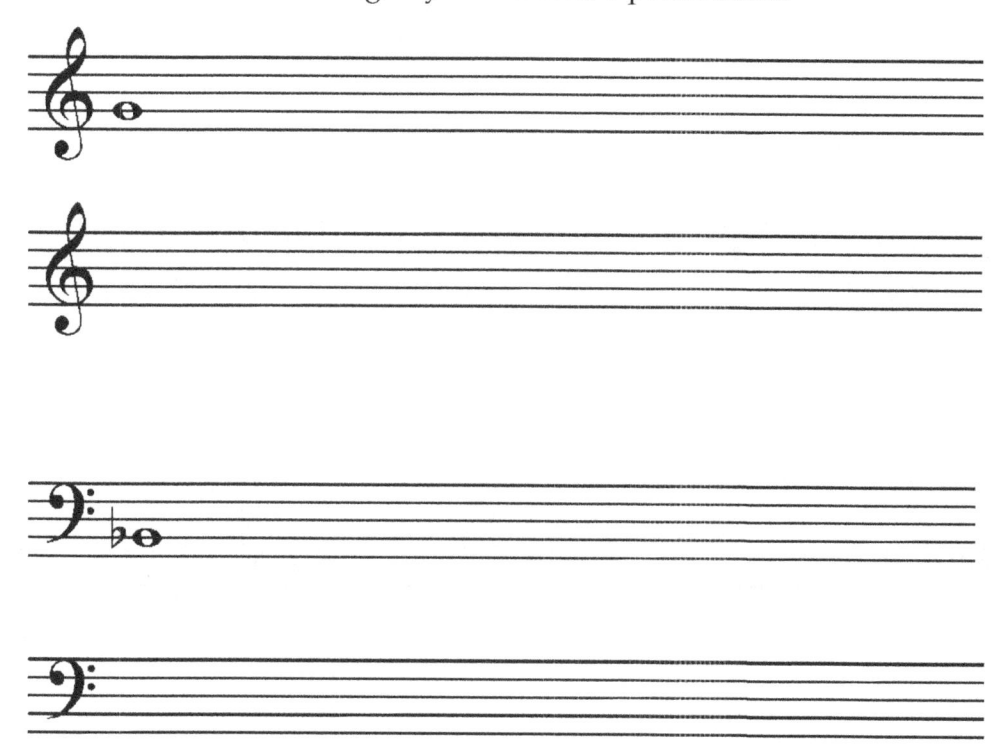

For each natural minor scale written below, add sharps, flats or naturals to create each scale variant. Then write in the solfege for your teacher's preferred system.
(Remember that the melodic minor scale is different ascending than it is descending.)

Harmonic Minor

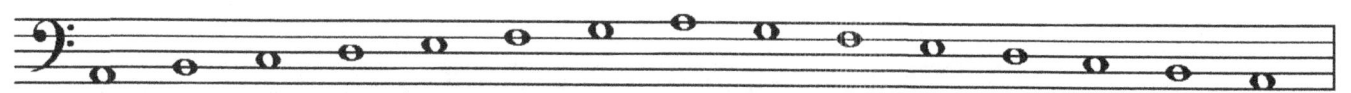

Melodic Minor

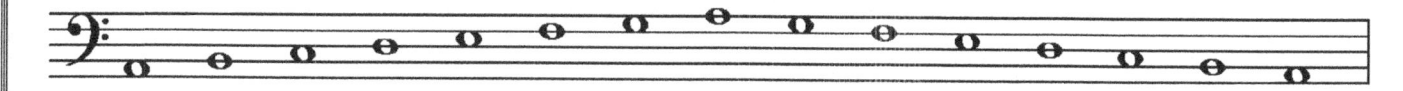

Sightreading 6

Each of the following examples is in a minor key. Throughout the exercises you will find moments where different variants of the minor scale are used. Take note of these pitch alterations (which will be on the 6th and 7th scale degrees) and use solfege accordingly.

1. Key of _____ minor

2. Key of _____ minor

3. Key of _____ minor

4. Key of _____ minor

Unit 2 Quiz

Complete the following sentences:

1. A _____ _____ is the interval when one note moves to the very next note, whether black or white.

2. The pattern of half and whole steps for the major scale is ___ ___ ___ ___ ___ ___ ___ .

3. The three types of minor scales are _____ , _____ , and _____ .

Identify each of the following key signatures:

____ Major   ____ Major   ____ Major   ____ Major

____ minor   ____ minor   ____ minor   ____ minor

Using the starting pitch provided, draw the correct scale using sharps, flats and naturals as needed.

1. Harmonic Minor - Ascending

2. Major – Descending

3. Melodic Minor - Ascending and Descending

Unit 3

- Lesson 7: Simple Meter vs. Compound Meter
- Lesson 8: Musical Road Signs
- Lesson 9: Interval Quality
- Unit 3 Quiz

Lesson 7
Simple Meter vs. Compound Meter

The time signatures we have focused on so far have been in **simple meter**. This means that the **beat subdivision**, the way the beats are split up into smaller note values, has been into two equal parts.

In the 4/4 example below, the first measure contains quarter notes, which each get one beat. In the second measure, the beats are divided into two eighth notes. Even with sixteenth notes added in the third measure, each beat can still be divided easily in half.

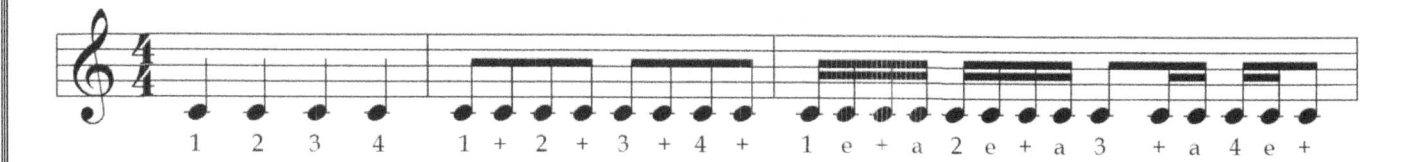

3/4 and 2/4 are also common examples of simple meter time signatures. They work the same way as 4/4 where the quarter note beat can be divided in half.

4/2 and 3/8 are other examples of time signatures in simple meter. In 4/2 the half note gets the beat, and the subdivision is the quarter note. In 3/8 the eighth note gets the beat, and the subdivision is the sixteenth note.

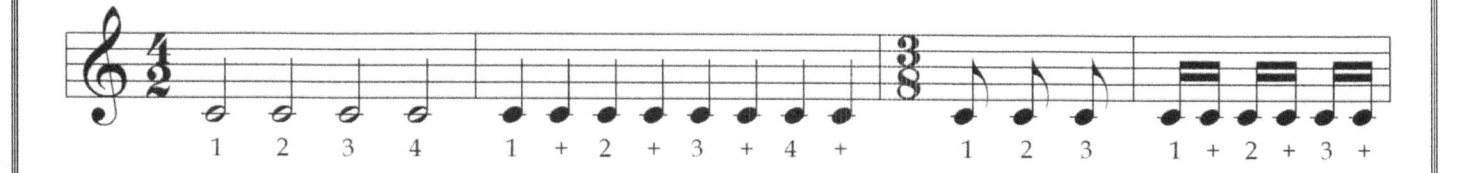

While time signatures using simple meter have beats that are divided in half, time signatures in **compound meter** have a beat that is divided into three equal parts and are said to have a subdivision of three.

One of the most common compound time signatures is 6/8. If you use the rule you learned before where the top note tells you the number of beats and the bottom number tells you what kind of note gets the beat, you might say that 6/8 has six beats and the eighth note gets the beat. 6/8 has six eighth notes per measure, but rather than counting six individual beats, it is more musical to count two big beats per measure, which are made up of three eighth notes.

In this case, the dotted quarter note gets the beat, and eighth notes are 1/3 of a beat. One way to count in compound meter is adding "la" "li" between beats.

Two other common compound time signatures are 9/8, which has three dotted quarter note beats per measure, and 12/8, which has 4 dotted quarter note beats per measure.

There are compound time signatures with other numbers on the bottom, such as 6/4, which has two dotted half note beats per measure with quarter note subdivisions, and 9/16, which has three dotted eighth note beats per measure with sixteenth note subdivisions.

A general rule for time signatures is that if the top number is 2, 3, or 4, it is simple meter, and if the top number is 6, 9, or 12, it is compound meter.

Worksheet 7
Simple Meter vs. Compound Meter

For each of the following time signatures, identify a) whether it is simple or compound, b) how many beats per measure there will be, c) what type of note gets the beat, and d) what type of note gets the subdivision.

Time Signature	Simple/Compound	Beats per Measure	One Beat =	Subdivision
4/4	Simple	4	♩	♪
6/8				
12/8				
3/2				
9/16				

a) Draw barlines between measures. b) Write the counts underneath. c) Label the key.

1. Key of _____

1 la li 2 la li 1 2 1 la li 2 la li 1 li 2

2. Key of _____

3. Key of _____

Sightreading 7

Determine whether each example is in compound meter or simple meter. If it is in compound meter, write the counts in underneath. Next, write the key. Be careful to check whether each melody is in the major key or its relative minor by examining the first and last note. (Music tends to start and end on the tonal center.) Finally, sing through each melody on solfege.

1 Key of _____

2 Key of _____

3 Key of _____

4 Key of _____

Lesson 8
Musical Road Signs

It is very common in a piece of music to have repeated material. Instead of writing out the same measures multiple times, composers will often use different "road signs" to direct the performer to go back to a section that has already been played or sung.

The most basic musical "road sign" is the **repeat sign**. It looks like a double bar line with two dots and instructs the musician to repeat the music they just played or sang. In the example below, after singing through the four-measure melody, the repeat sign instructs you to sing all four measures again.

Sometimes you will see a "backwards" repeat sign. Instead of returning to the very beginning, you would just return to the backwards repeat sign. In the case below, you would sing through all four measures and then repeat the last two measures.

Some repeats have 1st and 2nd endings, which are marked with "1." and "2." In the following example, you would go back to the beginning after the repeat sign. The second time through, you would skip the measure with the 1st ending and go straight to the 2nd ending.

Another marking you may come across is **D.C. al Fine. D.C.** stands for *"Da Capo,"* which means "from the head/beginning," and *"al Fine"* means "to the end." When you see this marking, you are to go back to the beginning of the piece and continue until you reach the **Fine** (pronounced "fee-nay"), which is the end of the piece.

D.S. al Fine is similar to D.C. al Fine. **D.S.** stands for *"Dal Segno"* and means "from the sign." Instead of going back to the very beginning, you would return to the sign that looks like a fancy *S* and then continue on to the Fine.

One additional marking is **D.C. al Coda**. **Coda** means "tail" in Italian and is an extra ending section. This means to go back to the beginning like a D.C. al Fine. When you reach the marking that says "To Coda" the second time, you skip ahead to the ending, which is marked Coda. It is also possible to have a **D.S. al Coda**.

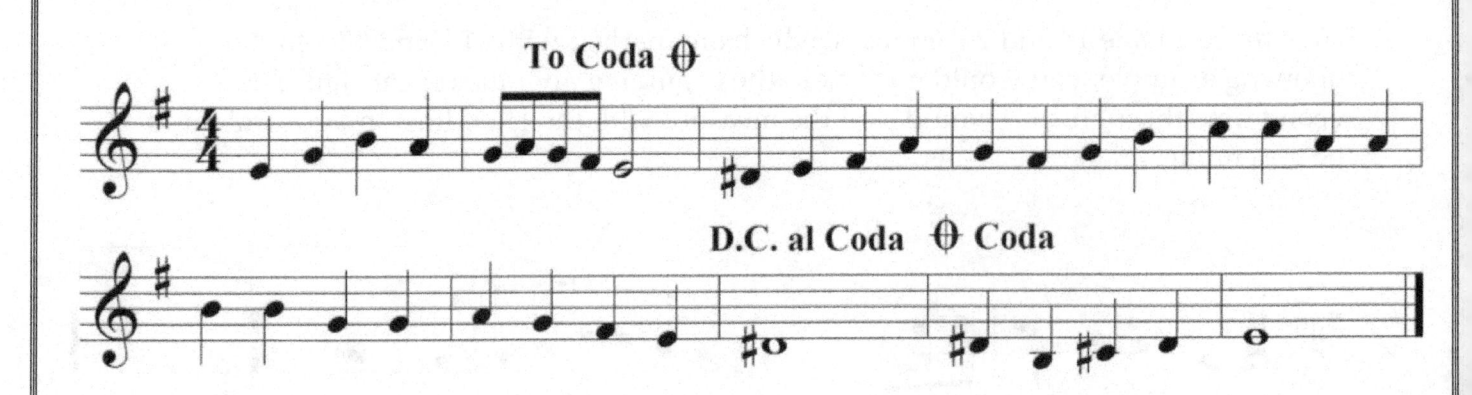

Worksheet 8
Musical Road Signs

Figure out a more efficient way to write these melodies using some of the "road signs" you just learned about.

1.

    a. What key is this example in? _____

    b. What is this key's relative minor? _____

    c. Does the time signature indicate simple or compound meter? _____

    d. What type of note receives one beat? _____

2.

    a. What key is this example in? _____

    b. What is this key's relative minor? _____

    c. Does the time signature indicate simple or compound meter? _____

    d. What type of note receives one beat? _____

Sometimes it is better to write out some repeats than to use too many "road signs" too close together. Rewrite the melody below without the "road signs."

a. What key is this example in? _____

b. What is this key's relative minor? _____

c. Does the time signature indicate simple or compound meter? _____

d. What type of note receives one beat? _____

Sightreading 8

Sing through each example on solfege. Be sure to follow all the musical "road signs" correctly.

1. Key of _____

2. Key of _____

3. Key of _____

4. Key of _____

Lesson 9
Interval Quality

In Lesson 4, you learned that the major scale is made up of a specific pattern of half and whole steps:

You also know that an interval is the distance between two notes. But did you know that intervals can be major, minor, perfect, diminished or augmented? These words refer to the **interval's quality**. For now we will discuss major, minor and perfect intervals.

We use the major scale to generate major and perfect intervals. The distance from "Do" to any other note in the major scale will give us either a major or perfect interval. We use a capital letter "M" to show that an interval is major and a capital letter "P" to show that an interval is perfect.

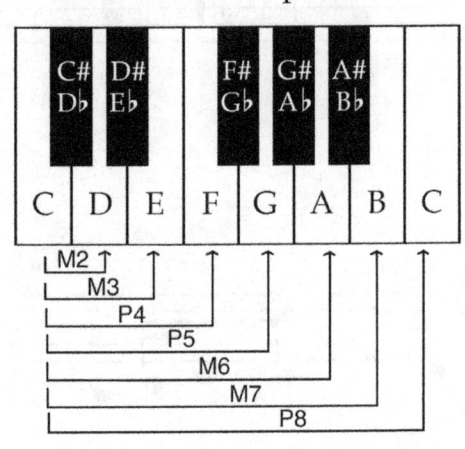

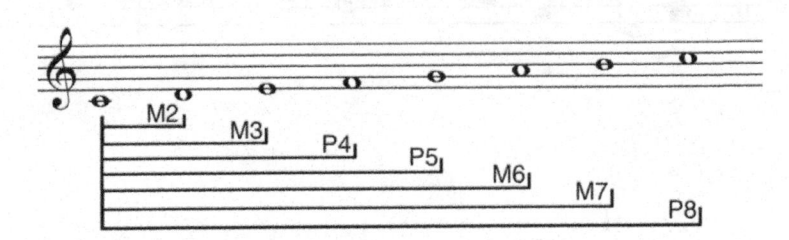

If we lower a Major interval by a half step, it becomes minor, which we show by using a lowercase "m." For example, C to Db is a minor second, or m2. C to Eb is a minor third, or m3.

To figure out the quality of an interval, you can either determine whether or not the top note is in the major key of the lower note or you can count the number of half steps from the bottom note to the top note. See the chart below for intervals up to a fifth:

Interval	Half Steps
m2	1
M2	2
m3	3
M3	4
P4*	5
P5*	7

*Note that 4ths and 5ths can also be diminished or augmented, but this book will focus only on Major, Minor, and Perfect intervals.

Worksheet 9
Interval Quality

Circle the correct answer:

1. In the key of C, C up to G is a **Perfect 4th** | **Perfect 5th**.

2. A minor second is the same as a **Half Step** | **Whole Step**.

3. A minor third is equal to **three** | **four** half steps.

4. To make a major interval minor, you must **raise** | **lower** the interval by a half step.

5. Major intervals are derived from the **minor** | **major** scale.

6. An interval's **distance** | **quality** refers to whether it is major, minor, perfect, augmented or diminished.

Identify each of the following harmonic intervals, including quality:

___ ___ ___ ___ ___ ___

Create each given melodic interval.

P4   m2   M2   m3   P5   M3

Review: Identify each Major key signature and provide the relative minor key.

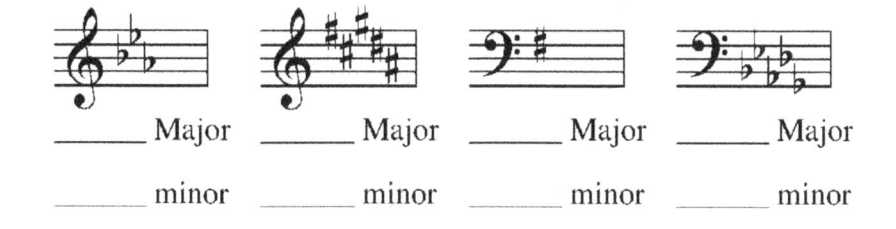

___ Major   ___ Major   ___ Major   ___ Major

___ minor   ___ minor   ___ minor   ___ minor

Sightreading 9

The following four examples are all in major keys and contain many skips. Before singing through on solfege, circle and label each interval greater than a 2nd including its quality.

[1] Key of _____

[2] Key of _____

[3] Key of _____

[4] Key of _____

Unit 3 Quiz

Complete the following sentences:

1. In compound meter, each beat is subdivided into _____ parts.

2. In 6/8 meter, the _____ _____ note establishes the beat.

3. This symbol :||) is called a _____ _____ .

4. In a piece of music, D.C. al Fine means to go back to the _____ and stop when you see *Fine*.

5. A major interval lowered by a half step is a _____ interval.

6. In the major scale, the interval from Do to Fa is a _____ _____ .

For the following musical excerpt, identify the intervals where indicated, specifying quality. Then, answer the questions below.

m3

a. This excerpt is in the key of _____ _____ .

b. Is this example in simple meter or compound meter? _____

c. Including the repeat and endings, the musician would end up playing _____ total measures.

d. Noting the time signature, the total number of beats in this example is _____ .

e. The notes in the second ending are derived from the _____ form of the minor scale.

Unit 4

- Lesson 10: Introduction to Chords
- Lesson 11: Intervals Greater than a 5th
- Lesson 12: Tonic and Dominant
- Unit 4 Quiz

Lesson 10
Introduction to Chords

In Level 1, you learned that when two or more notes are played or sung together, the result is called harmony. When three or more notes combine to make a single harmonic sound, the result is a **chord**. A chord with exactly three pitches is called a **triad.**

The simplest triads are built by stacking two thirds on top of each other:

Notice that on the staff, these chords look like snowmen. Each is built on either three line notes or three space notes.

Each of these three chord members has a name. The **root** is the bottom note of the snowman; the **third** is the middle note, and the **fifth** is the top note.

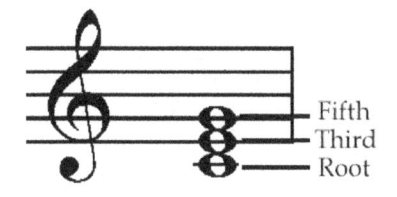

You will find chords in two forms. **Block chords** occur when all the notes of that chord are played or sung simultaneously. **Broken chords** occur when the notes are played one at a time.

Block   Broken

Much like intervals, chords can be described as major, minor, augmented, or diminished. For now, we will focus on major and minor chords. A **major chord**, much like a major scale, sounds bright and happy. A chord is major if it contains a major third on the bottom and a minor third on the top. A **minor chord**, like a minor scale, sounds dark and sad. A chord is minor if it contains a minor third on the bottom and a major third on the top.

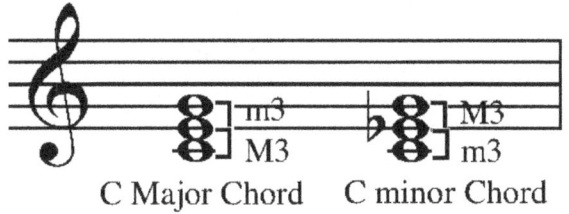

C Major Chord   C minor Chord

39

Worksheet 10
Introduction to Chords

Complete the following sentences:

1. A _____ is three or more notes that combine together to make one harmonic sound. One that has exactly three notes is called a _____ .

2. In "snowman position," the lowest note is called the _____ ; the middle note is called the _____ , and the top note is called the _____ .

Use each given pitch as the root and build a triad.

Determine whether each chord is Major (M) or minor (m).
*Remember, a major chord has a major third (M3) on the bottom and a minor chord has a minor third (m3) on the bottom.

Review: *For each of the following time signatures, circle "Simple" or "Compound" and draw the type of note that gets the beat.*

$^6_8$	$^3_4$	$^9_8$	$^6_4$	$^3_2$	$^4_{16}$
Simple/ Compound	Simple/ Compound	Simple/ Compound	Simple/ Compound	Simple/ Compound	Simple/ Compound

Sightreading 10

The following examples contain many broken triads. Circle the triads then sing through each example with your teacher.

1 Key of _____

2 Key of _____

3 Key of _____

4 Key of _____

Lesson 11
Intervals Greater than a 5th

In Lesson 9, you learned that intervals such as 2nds and 3rds can be major or minor and 4ths and 5ths can be perfect, diminished, or augmented. Let us explore some of the intervals larger than a 5th. If you get used to the sound and appearance of each interval, you will have no trouble sightreading examples with lots of skips.

An interval larger than a 5th is a 6th. On the staff, a 6th is a large skip from a line to a space or a space to a line. Just like 2nds and 3rds, 6ths can be major or minor. When singing, some common major 6ths are "do" to "la" or "sol" to "mi." Some common minor sixths are "do" to "le" or "sol" to "me."

The 7th is a large skip from a line to a line or a space to a space and can be major or minor. Singing "do" up to "ti" is a common major 7th and "sol" to "fa" is a common minor 7th.

The 8th, also known as the octave, is a skip from one note to the next note of the same name, such as A to A or E to E. 8ths are perfect intervals, not major or minor. It is possible to have diminished and augmented 8ths like 4ths and 5ths, but these are very uncommon.

Did you know?

Intervals that are larger than an octave are called **compound intervals** because they are the same as another interval plus an octave. For example, if you sing C and then D right next to it, you will sing a major 2nd. You could also sing C to D with an octave in between, which would be a major 9th or an octave plus a 2nd.

Worksheet 11
Intervals Greater than 5ths

Label each interval including its quality: Major (M), minor (m), or Perfect (P)
Remember, to figure out the quality of an interval, determine whether or not the top note is in the major key of the lower note. If yes, the interval is major or perfect. An interval that is a half step smaller than a major interval is minor.

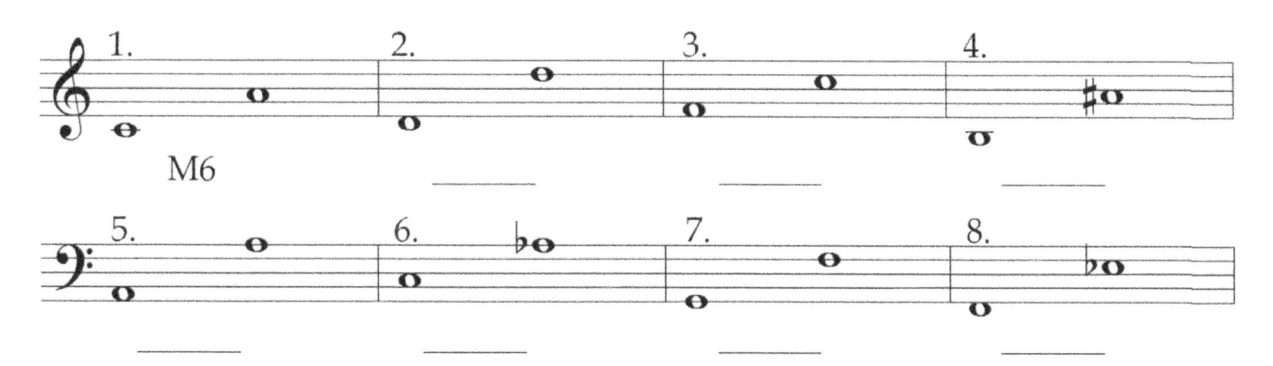

1. M6   2. ____   3. ____   4. ____

5. ____   6. ____   7. ____   8. ____

Write the note above each note to form the correct interval.

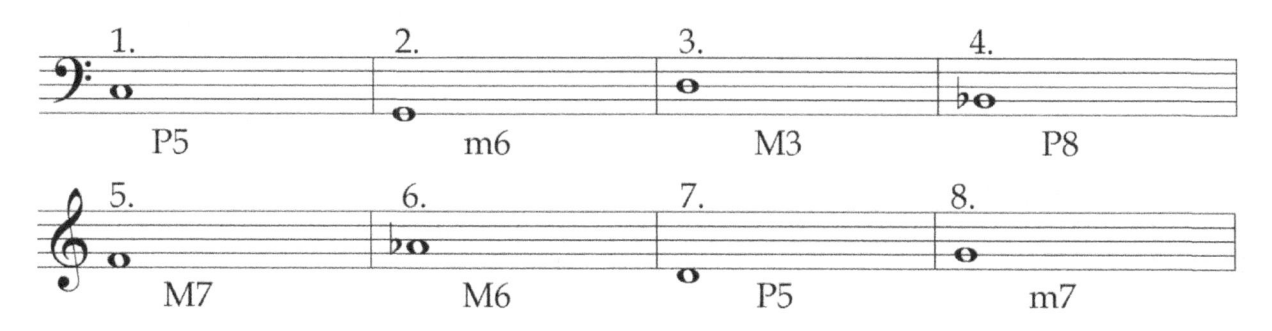

1. P5   2. m6   3. M3   4. P8

5. M7   6. M6   7. P5   8. m7

1. A 6th **above** "do" is _____.
2. A 7th **above** "sol" is _____.
3. An 8th **above** "re" is _____.
4. A 3rd **above** "fa" is _____.
5. A 6th **above** "la" is _____.

6. A 2nd **below** "mi" is _____.
7. A 7th **below** "ti" is _____.
8. An 8th **below** "la" is _____.
9. A 4th **below** "fa" is _____.
10. A 6th **below** "sol" is _____.

Sightreading 11

Circle and label any skips of 6ths, 7ths, or 8ths, and then sing through each example on solfege.

1 Key of _____

2 Key of _____

3 Key of _____

4 Key of _____

Lesson 12
Tonic and Dominant

In Lesson 10, you learned how to build a chord or triad. It is possible to build a chord on every note of the scale. When you do this, some of the chords will be major, and some will be minor. Each chord is assigned a Roman numeral. The chord built on "do" is "I," on "re" is "ii," on "mi" is "iii," etc.

The upper case Roman numeral chords are major, and the lower case Roman numeral chords are minor. If you build these chords on a major scale, I, IV, and V are major, and ii, iii, and vi are minor. (The vii° chord is diminished, which is a type of chord we haven't learned about yet.)

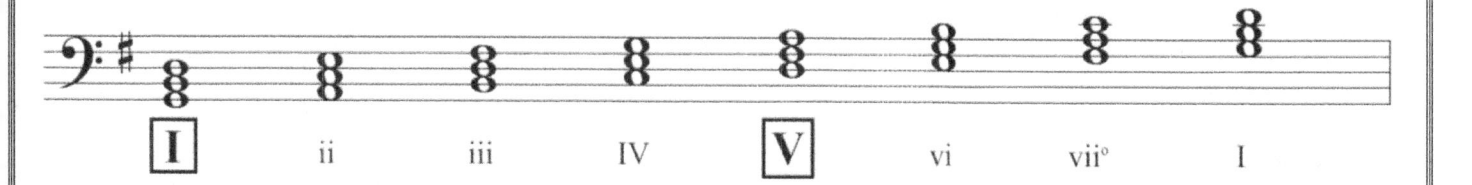

For now, we will focus on the I chord and the V chord, which are also known as **tonic** and **dominant**, respectively. These are probably the most common chords in tonal music, and many songs can be harmonized using just these two chords.

The tonic chord (I) is always the chord built on the first scale degree (or "do") and is "home base" for the key. Most pieces begin and end on the I chord, and when you hear this chord, the music sounds like it is in a stable place. You can see some tonic chords written below. In the key of C, C is tonic; in the key of A♭, A♭ is tonic; in the key of F#, F# is tonic.

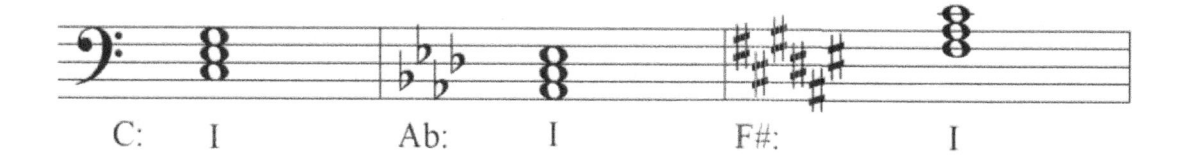

The dominant chord (V) is built on the fifth scale degree (or "sol"). The dominant chord is a less stable chord than tonic and "wants" to resolve back to I. The following figure shows a few examples of the V chord in different keys. In the key of C, G is dominant; in the key of A♭, E♭ is dominant; in the key of F#, C# is dominant.

When deciding what chords to harmonize a melody with, it is generally best to use a chord that contains some of the melody notes. In the following example, measures 1, 2, and 4 are mostly made up of notes that are in the I chord, and measure 3 has D, which is in the V chord.

Worksheet 12
Tonic and Dominant

Write the correct key signature; then build the tonic and dominant chords.

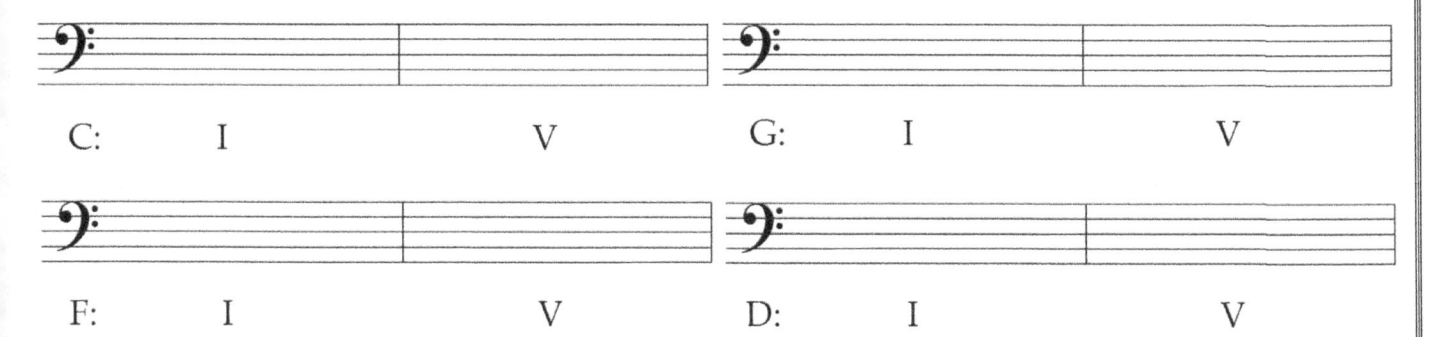

C: I   V   G: I   V

F: I   V   D: I   V

Label the tonic (I) and dominant (V) chords in the following examples:

Key of ____

Key of ____

1) Label the key and write the appropriate time signature. 2) Decide which chords would go well with the following melody. 3) Write the chords in the bass clef staff, and label the Roman numerals underneath. **Note:** there is not a single "right answer."

Key of ____

Sightreading 12

Label the I and V chords that accompany each melody, and then sing through on solfege as your teacher plays the chords on the piano.

[1] Key of _____

[2] Key of _____

[3] Key of _____

Unit 4 Quiz

Answer the following questions:

1. A major third with a minor third stacked on top is called a _____ _____.

2. A minor third with a major third stacked on top is called a _____ _____.

3. The interval a half step smaller than a Major 6th is a _____ _____ .

4. The interval a half step larger than a Major 3rd is a _____ _____ .

5. The interval from Do up to Ti is a _____ _____ .

6. In any key, the tonic chord is given the Roman numeral ____ .

7. In any key, the _____ chord is given the Roman numeral V.

8. In the key of G Major, the dominant (V) chord is ____ .

9. In the key of B♭ Major, the tonic (I) chord is _____ .

Using the given note as a root, build each triad with the indicated quality.

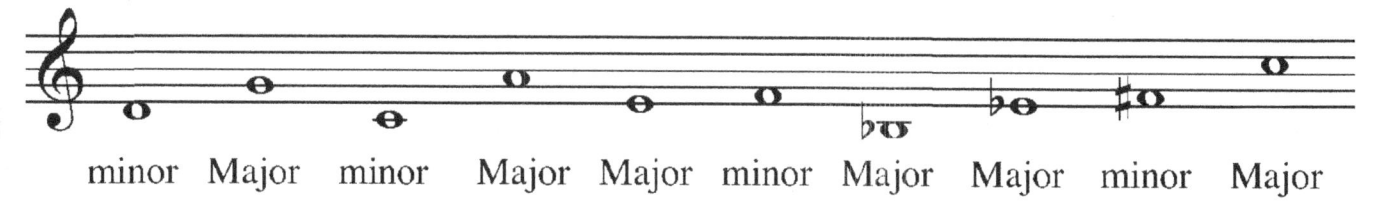

minor   Major   minor   Major   Major   minor   Major   Major   minor   Major

Draw the following ascending intervals from the given note:

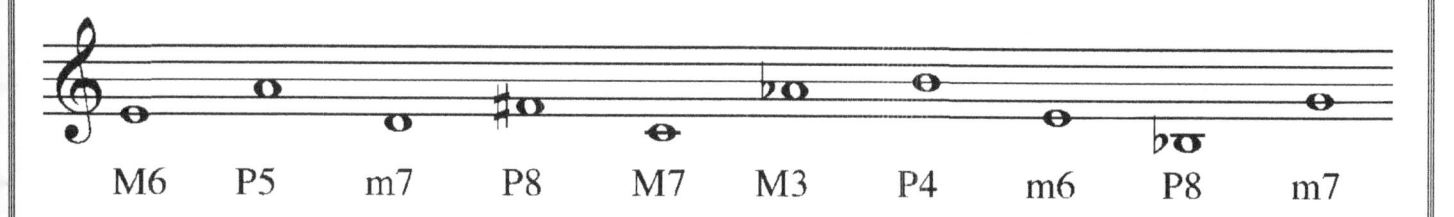

M6   P5   m7   P8   M7   M3   P4   m6   P8   m7

Unit 5

- Lesson 13: Supertonic and Subdominant
- Lesson 14: The Chromatic Scale
- Lesson 15: Roman Numerals in Minor
- Unit 5 Quiz

Lesson 13
Supertonic and Subdominant

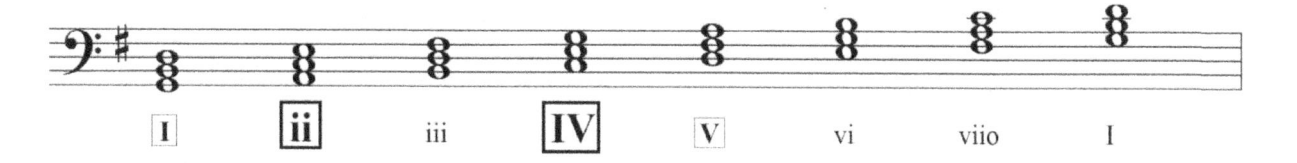

I   ii   iii   IV   V   vi   viio   I

After I and V, the IV chord, also known as **subdominant**, is the next most commonly used chord. Any note in the major scale can fit into one of these three chords, so it is easy to harmonize an entire song with them. *Note that certain notes fit into more than one chord. For example, the root of a I chord is "do," which is also the 5th of IV chord.

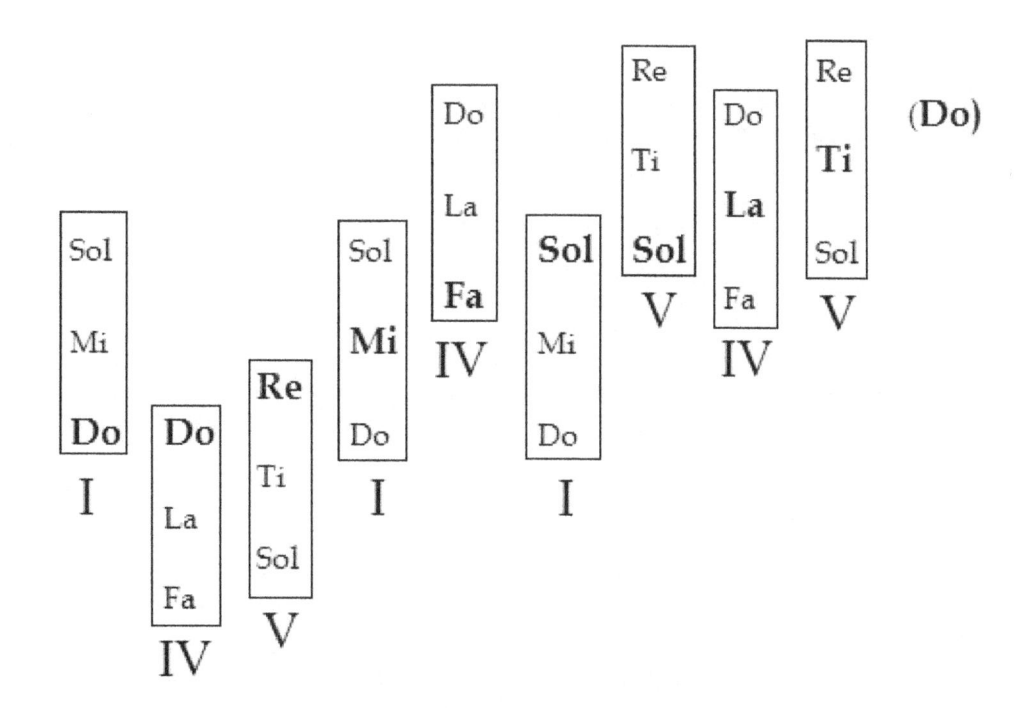

The ii chord, also known as **supertonic**, is a minor chord built on the second degree of a major scale. The solfege syllables for the ii chord are "re" "fa" "la."

In a sequence of chords (or **chord progression**), IV and ii often act to prepare the ear for the V chord. They are called **predominants** because they come before the dominant chord. Remember that the V chord is less stable and wants to resolve back to I. Two very common chord progressions are I → IV → V → I and I → ii → V → I.

*Note that the IV chord and the ii chord share two of the same pitches ("fa" and "la"), so they can often be used interchangeably.

Worksheet 13
Supertonic and Subdominant

Write the correct key signature; then build the given chords.

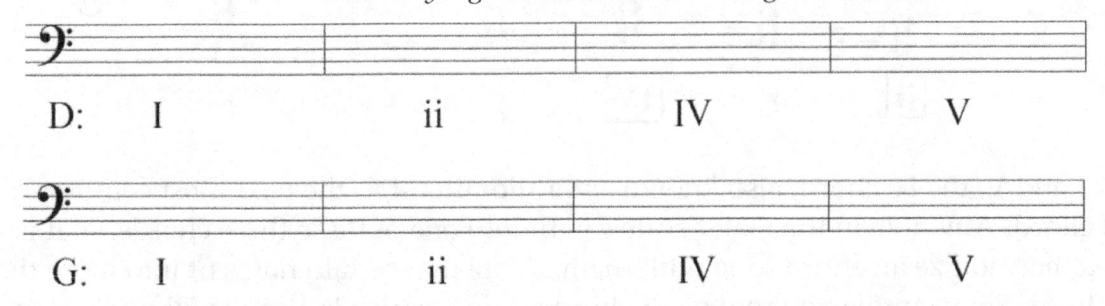

D: I   ii   IV   V

G: I   ii   IV   V

Label the chords in the following example with Roman numerals:

Key of _____

Decide which chords would go well with the following melody. Write the chords in the bass clef staff, and label the Roman numerals underneath. **Note:** *there is not a single "right answer."*

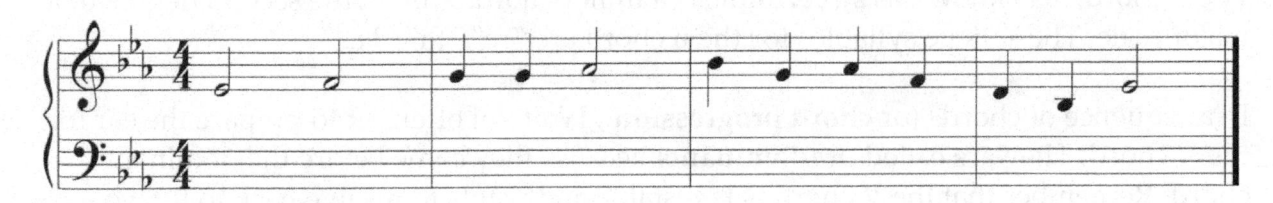

Review: *Identify each of the following intervals, including its quality (M, m or P)*

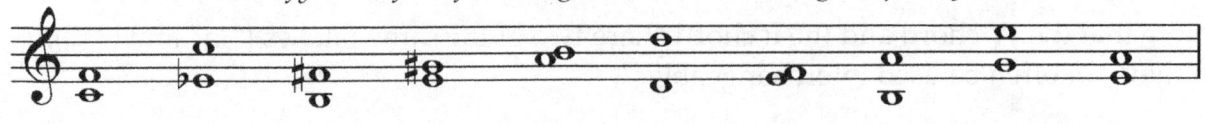

Sightreading 13

Label the chords that accompany each melody with Roman numerals, and then sing through each melody on solfege as your teacher plays the chords on the piano.

1 Key of _____

2 Key of _____

3 Key of _____

Lesson 14
The Chromatic Scale

You already know that a scale is a collection of notes. So far you have learned about the major scale as well as three forms of the minor scale. Another type of scale is the **chromatic scale**, which is a succession of notes, all a half step apart. Imagine if you were to play every note on the piano one at a time without skipping any. You would have played a gigantic chromatic scale.

Below is an ascending chromatic scale starting and ending on C. Note the half steps between each pitch.

While it is rare that you will ever sing a chromatic scale like the one above in a piece of music, we use this scale to learn some of the variations of solfege that you might encounter. In fact, we use the word **chromatic** to describe notes that are not found in a particular key or scale. These notes are easy to identify because they have an added sharp, flat, or natural.

The solfege for an ascending chromatic scale is different from that of a descending chromatic scale. When singing an ascending chromatic scale, each vowel is changed to an "ee" sound to show that it is a half-step higher:

Do Di Re Ri Mi Fa Fi Sol Si La Li Ti Do

When singing a descending chromatic scale, the vowels are changed to an "eh" sound except for "re," which becomes "ra." You may recognize some of these syllables from the natural minor scale:

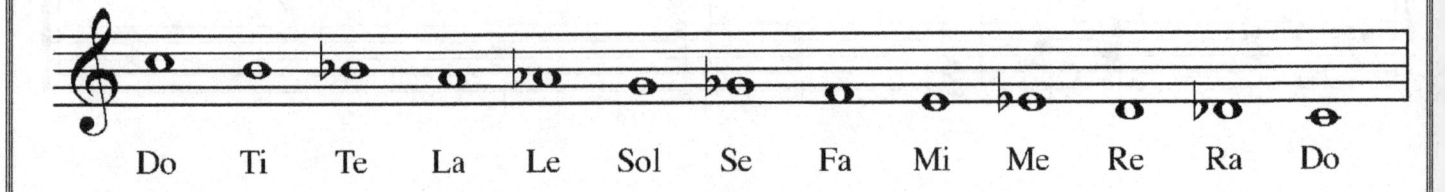

Do Ti Te La Le Sol Se Fa Mi Me Re Ra Do

Worksheet 14
The Chromatic Scale

Using the given note as a starting pitch, build an ascending chromatic scale. Then write the correct solfege under each note.

Using the given note as a starting pitch, build a descending chromatic scale. Then write the correct solfege under each note.

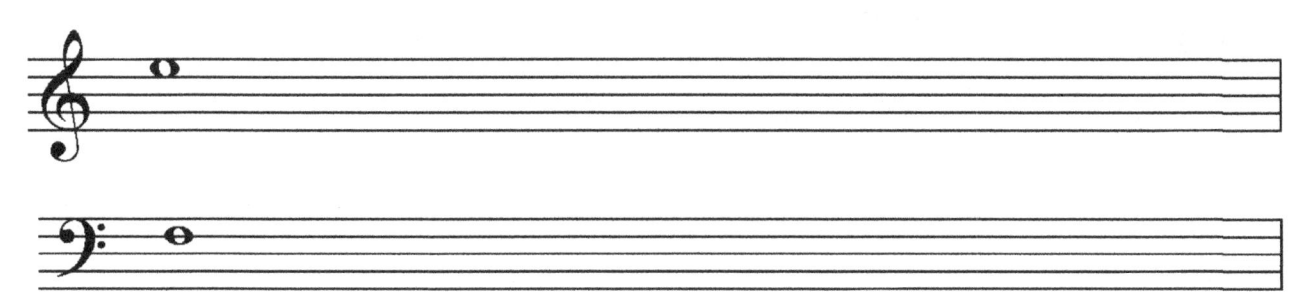

Answer the following questions.

1. The note a half step lower than Re is _____ .

2. Le raised by a half step is _____ .

3. In the key of C, the solfege for the note F# is _____ .

4. In the key of D, "Ra" would be the note _____ .

Review: *Identify each of the following intervals, including its quality (M, m or P)*

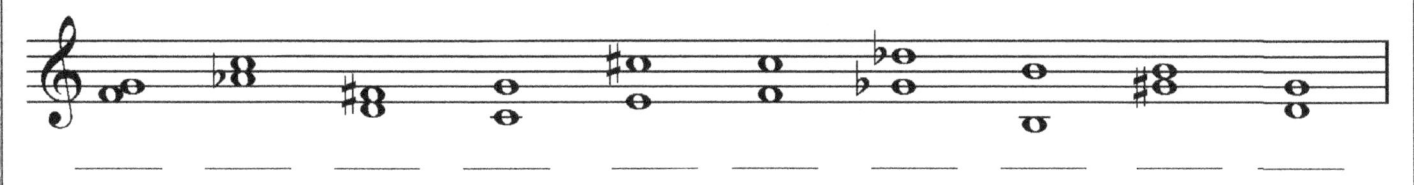

Sightreading 14

Each of the following examples contains several chromatic pitches. Be sure to use the appropriate chromatic solfege.

1. Key of _____

2. Key of _____

3. Key of _____

4. Key of _____

Lesson 15
Roman Numerals in Minor

Just like in major, chords can be built on each scale degree in the minor scale. Since the minor scale is based on a different pattern of whole steps and half steps, the chord qualities are different than those in a major key. See the example below for the chords in the key of A minor:

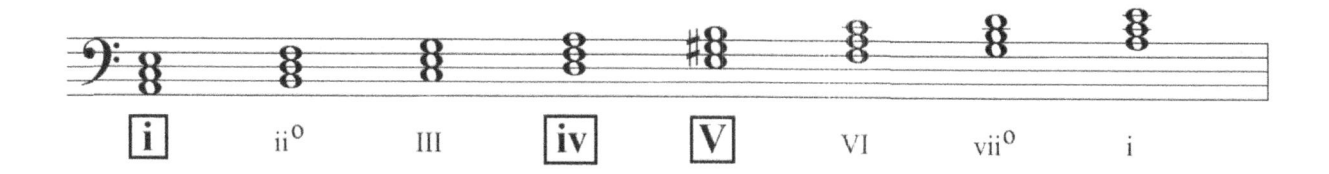

i   ii°   III   iv   V   VI   vii°   i

The chords we will focus on for minor keys are tonic, subdominant, and dominant. As you can see above, the tonic and subdominant chords (i and iv) are minor and the dominant chord (V) is major.

Notice that the V chord has a G# and not a G natural. G# is the raised 7th (or "ti") in the key of A minor, which is present in the harmonic form of the minor scale. The harmonic minor scale was developed for this very purpose: to make the V chord major in a minor key, which gives it a stronger pull back towards tonic. The raised 7th is also called the **leading tone** and is just a half step away from tonic. This half step distance makes the leading tone tend to *lead* to tonic.

Below are examples of i, iv, and V in different minor keys. Notice that the raised 7th is not always a sharp. Depending on the key signature, it could also be a natural, like in C minor where the B♭ is raised to a B natural.

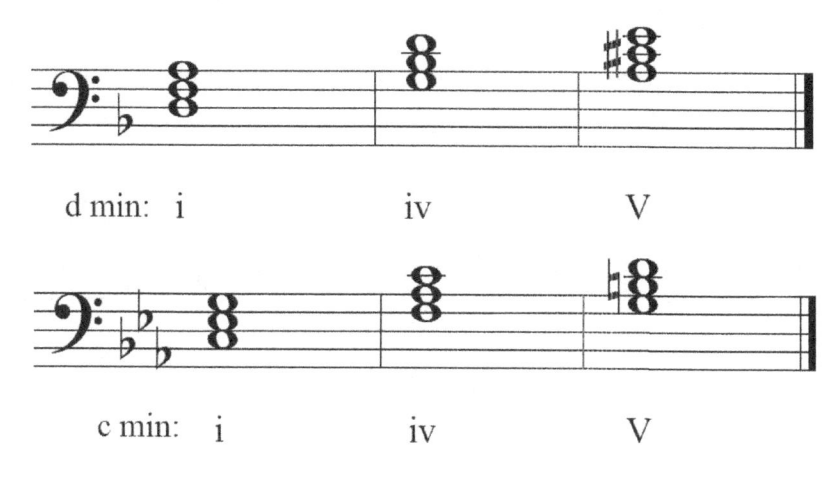

d min: i   iv   V

c min: i   iv   V

Worksheet 15
Roman Numerals in Minor

Write the correct key signature; then write the given chords.

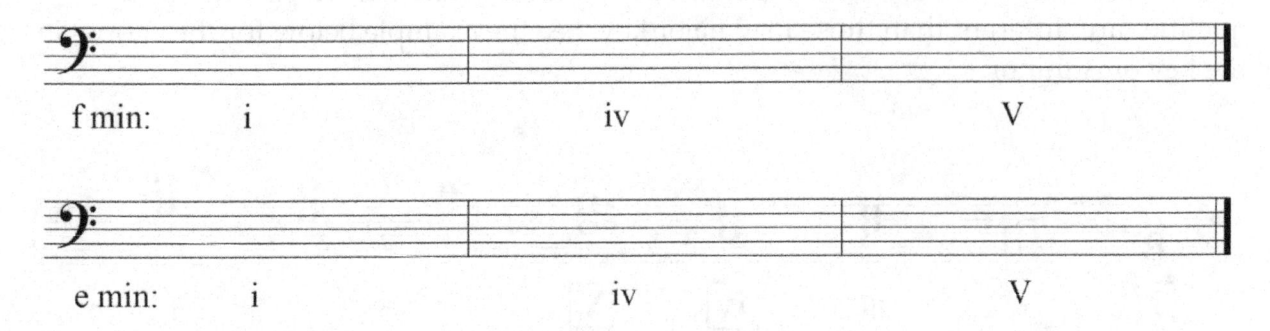

f min:　　　i　　　　　　　　　iv　　　　　　　　　V

e min:　　　i　　　　　　　　　iv　　　　　　　　　V

Label the chords in the following example with Roman numerals:

Key of _____

Decide which chords would go well with the following melody. Write the chords in the bass clef staff, and label the Roman numerals underneath. **Note:** *there is not a single "right answer."*

Key of _____

Sightreading 15

Label chords that accompany each melody with Roman numerals, and then sing through on solfege as your teacher plays the chords on the piano. Be sure to determine whether each example is in a major key or a minor key.

1 Key of _____

2 Key of _____

3 Key of _____

Unit 5 Quiz

Answer the following questions:

1. The IV chord is also known as the _____ chord.

2. The supertonic chord is represented by the Roman Numeral _____ .

3. We use the word _____ to describe notes that are not found in a particular key or scale.

4. In a minor key, the quality of the tonic and subdominant chords is _____ .

5. The dominant chord in a minor key is usually Major because it contains the

    _____ _____, or raised 7th scale degree.

In the example below, do the following:

a. Determine the key.
b. Fill in the missing quarter notes using the intervals indicated.
c. Choose chords that fit the melody from the ones you have studied.
d. Build those chords in the bass clef staff.
e. Label the Roman numerals for the chords you have chosen.

Key of _____

Final Review

Complete the following sentences:

1. Music that is bright and happy like most Christmas music is in a _____ key.

2. Music that has a dark, sad quality is in a _____ key.

3. Two keys that share the same key signature but have different tonal centers are called _____.

4. The pattern of half and whole steps for the major scale is ___ ___ ___ ___ ___ ___ ___.

5. The three types of minor scales are _____, _____, and _____.

6. In simple meter, each beat is subdivided into _____ parts.

7. In compound meter, each beat is subdivided into _____ parts.

8. In 6/8 meter, the _____ _____ note establishes the beat.

9. This symbol (:||) is called a _____ _____.

10. A major interval lowered by a half step is a _____ interval.

11. A _____ chord has a major third with a minor third stacked on top.

12. A minor chord has a _____ third with a major third stacked on top.

13. In any key, the _____ chord is given the Roman numeral I.

14. In any key, the dominant chord is given the Roman numeral _____.

15. The IV chord is also known as the _____ chord.

16. The supertonic chord is represented by the Roman numeral _____.

17. We use the word _____ to describe notes that are not found in a particular key or scale.

Identify the following key signatures:

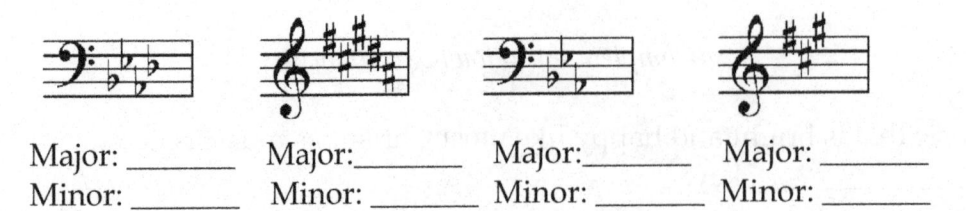

Major: _____   Major: _____   Major: _____   Major: _____
Minor: _____   Minor: _____   Minor: _____   Minor: _____

Note the time signature and add barlines to the following example. Don't forget to add a double barline at the end.

Using the starting pitch provided, draw the correct scale using sharps, flats and naturals as needed.

1. Harmonic Minor - Ascending

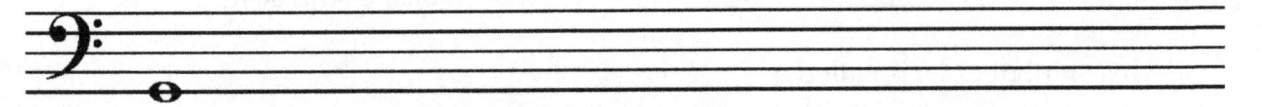

2. Major – Descending

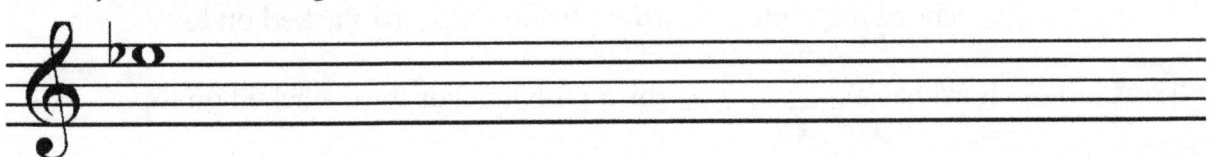

Build triads on each of the following notes with the given quality.

minor   Major   minor   Major   Major   minor   Major   Major   minor   Major

Use the directions below, which will guide you through a well-known tune.

First, write out the melody on the treble clef staff.

Measure 1: (two half notes)
- Start on Do.
- Go up an octave.

Measure 2: (quarter, 2 eighths, 2 quarters)
- Go down a half step.
- Go down a 3rd.
- Go up to La.
- Write the same note as the first beat.
- Go up to Do.

Measure 3: (two half notes)
- Go down an octave.
- Go up a sixth.

Measure 4: (whole note)
- Go down to Sol.

Measure 5: (two half notes)
- Go down a 7th
- Go up a 6th

Measure 6: (quarter, 2 eighths, 2 quarters)
- Go down to Mi.
- Go down a 3rd.
- Go up to Re.
- Write the same note as the first beat.
- Go up to Fa.

Measure 7: (quarter, 2 eighths, 2 quarters)
- Write the same as Measure 6 except move all notes down a whole step.

Measure 8: (whole note)
- Write the same note as beat one of Measure 1.

Once you've written out the melody, add chords in the left hand that you think would go well with the melody and label them with Roman numerals.

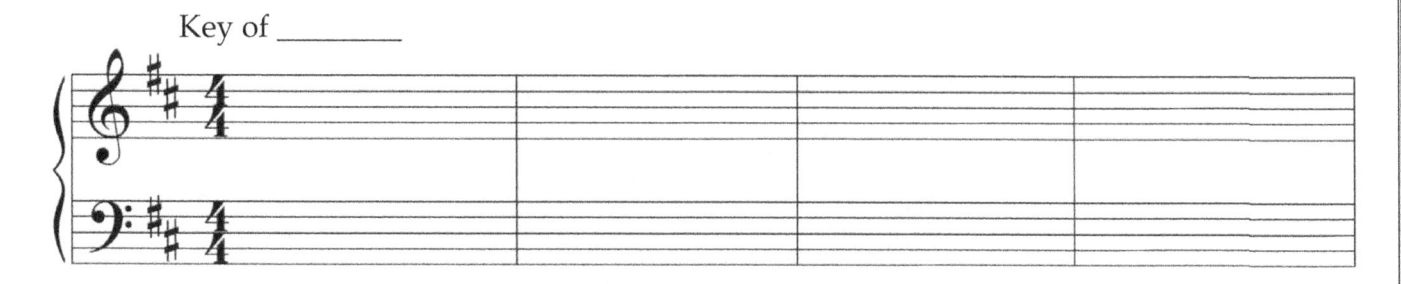

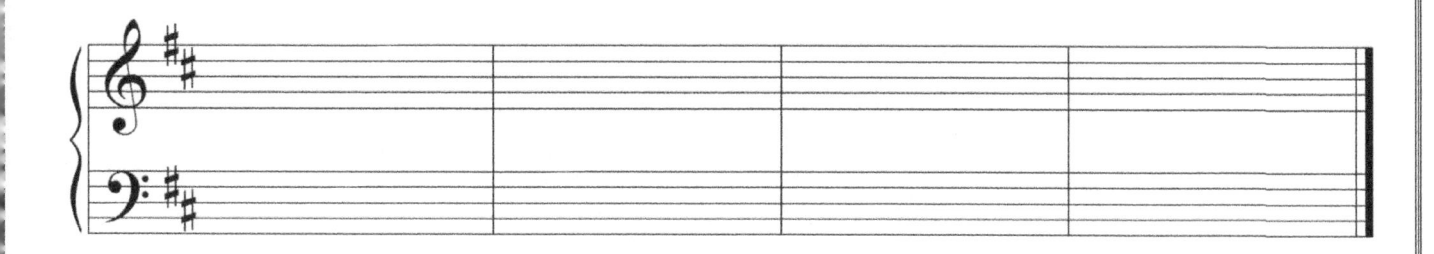

Key of _____

Appendix A
Key Signatures

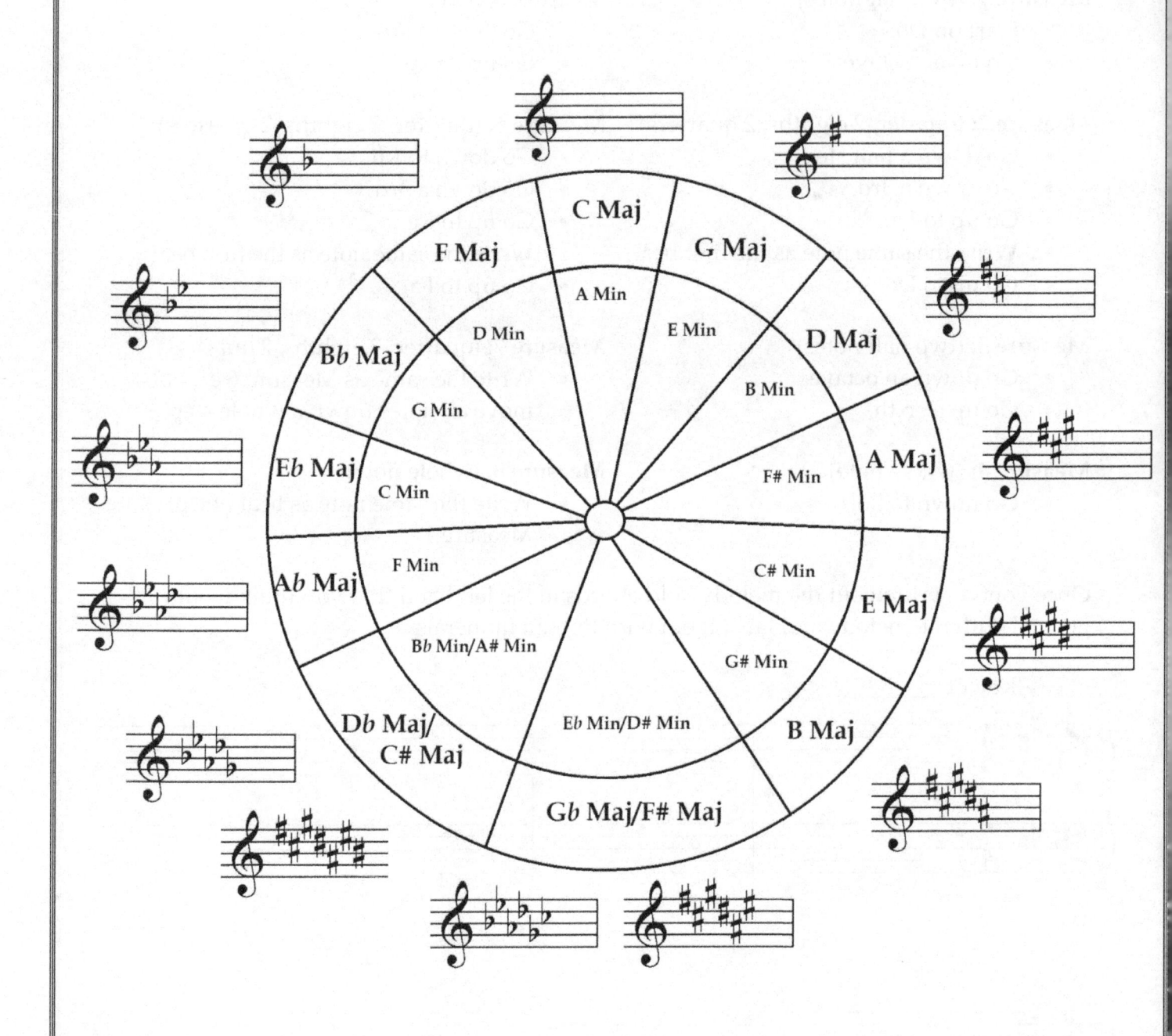

Appendix B
Scales

Major:

W W H W W W H

Do Re Mi Fa Sol La Ti Do

Natural Minor:

W H W W H W W

La Ti Do Re Mi Fa Sol La
Do Re Me Fa Sol Le Te Do

Harmonic Minor:

Raised 7th

La Ti Do Re Mi Fa Si La
Do Re Me Fa Sol Le Ti Do

Melodic Minor:

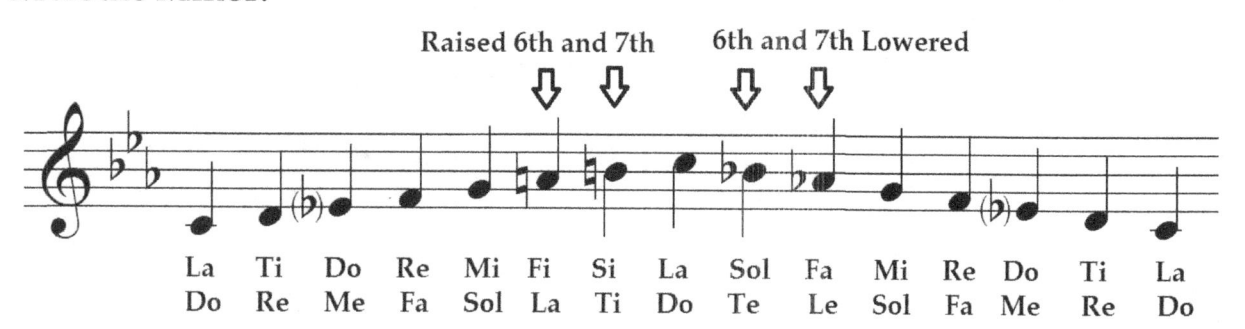

Raised 6th and 7th   6th and 7th Lowered

La Ti Do Re Mi Fi Si La Sol Fa Mi Re Do Ti La
Do Re Me Fa Sol La Ti Do Te Le Sol Fa Me Re Do

Major Scales

Minor Scales (Natural Form)

Glossary

Beat Subdivision-the way beats are split up into smaller note values. (Lesson 7)

Block Chord-all the notes of the chord are struck simultaneously. (Lesson 10)

Broken Chord-notes of the chord are played individually. (Lesson 10)

Chord-when three or more notes combine to make a single harmonic sound. (Lesson 10)

Chord Progression-a sequence of chords. (Lesson 13)

Chromatic-a word used to describe pitches that are not found in a particular key or scale. (Lesson 14)

Chromatic Scale-a succession of notes, all a half step apart. (Lesson 14)

Coda-an extra ending section. (Lesson 8)

Compound Interval-an interval larger than an octave. (Lesson 11)

Compound Meter-a time signature that divides beats into three equal parts. (Lesson 7)

D.C.-abbreviation for *"Da Capo,"* meaning "from the head/beginning." (Lesson 8)

D.C. al Coda-a musical marking indicating that the player return to the beginning and when he reaches the "To Coda" marking the second time to skip ahead to the "Coda" at the end of the piece. (Lesson 8)

D.C. al Fine-a musical marking indicating that the player return to the beginning of the piece and continue until he reaches the Fine. (Lesson 8)

Dominant-the fifth note of a scale or the chord built on the fifth note of a scale. (Lesson 12)

D.S.-abbreviation for *"Dal Segno,"* meaning "from the sign." (Lesson 8)

D.S. al Fine-a music marking indicating that the player return to the "*S*" sign and continue playing until he reaches the "Fine" marking. (Lesson 8)

D.S. al Coda-a musical marking indicating that the player return to the "*S*" sign and continue playing until he reaches the "To Coda" marking . At this point, he skips to the coda. (Lesson 8)

Fifth-the top note of a triad in "snowman position." (Lesson 10)

Fine-the end of a piece. (Lesson 8)

Half Step-movement from one note to the very next note, same as a minor 2nd. (Lesson 4)

Harmonic Minor Scale-the minor scale that raises the 7th scale degree. (Lesson 6)

Interval Quality-a word used to refer to whether an interval is major, minor, perfect, diminished, or augmented. (Lesson 9)

Key Signature-a set of sharps of flats that denotes the key of a piece of music. (Lesson 3)

Leading Tone-the 7th scale degree when it is a half step lower than tonic. (Lesson 15)

Ledger Line-a special line used for notes written below or above the staff. (Lesson 1)

Major 2nd-movement from one note to another with exactly one note in between, same as a whole step. (Lesson 4)

Major Chord-a triad built with a major third on the bottom and a minor third on top. (Lesson 10)

Major Scale-a collection of pitches with a particular combination of whole steps and half steps (W, W, H, W, W, W, H). (Lesson 4)

Melodic Minor Scale-the minor scale that raises the 6th and 7th scale degrees ascending and lowers them descending. (Lesson 6)

Minor 2nd-movement from one note to the very next note, same as a half step. (Lesson 4)

Minor Chord-a triad built with a minor third on the bottom and a major third on top. (Lesson 10)

Minor Scale-a collection of pitches with a particular combination of whole steps and half steps (W, H, W, W, H, W, W). (Lesson 5)

Natural Minor Scale-the minor scale that uses only the notes found in the key signature. (Lesson 6)

Natural Sign-a marking that cancels out a sharp or flat. (Lesson 6)

Predominant-a chord that is used to lead to the dominant (V) chord. (Lesson 13)

Relative Minor-a minor key that shares the same key signature with a major key. (Lesson 5)

Repeat Sign-a musical marking indicating that a section is to be played or sung again. (Lesson 8)

Root-the bottom note of a triad in "snowman position." (Lesson 10)

Scale-a collection of pitches. (Lesson 4)

Simple Meter-a time signature that divides beats into two equal parts. (Lesson 7)

Sixteenth Note-a note that last one quarter of a beat. (Lesson 2)

Subdominant-the fourth note of a scale or the chord built on the fourth note of a scale. (Lesson 13)

Supertonic-the second note of a scale or the chord built on the second note of a scale. (Lesson 13)

Third-the middle note of a triad in "snowman position." (Lesson 10)

Tie-a curved line that joins together two or more notes on the same line or space, causing them to be held for the value of the notes added together. (Lesson 2)

Tonal Center-the note of a key that feels like home or "Do." (Lesson 6)

Tonic-the first note of a scale or the chord built on the first note of a scale. (Lesson 12)

Triad-a chord with exactly three pitches. (Lesson 10)

Whole Step-movement from one note to another with exactly one note in between, same as a Major 2nd. (Lesson 4)

Made in the USA
Las Vegas, NV
06 November 2023